THE 10

Most Outstanding Canadian Symbols

Karen Dick • Robert Cutting

Series Editor
Jeffrey D. Wilhelm

Much thought, debate, and research went into choosing and ranking the 10 items in each book in this series. We realize that everyone has his or her own opinion of what is most significant, revolutionary, amazing, deadly, and so on. As you read, you may agree with our choices, or you may be surprised — and that's the way it should be!

SCHOLASTIC
www.scholastic.ca/education

175 Hillmount Road
Markham, Ontario
L6C 1Z7

A Rubicon book published in association with Scholastic Canada

Ru'bicon © 2007 Rubicon Publishing Inc.
www.rubiconpublishing.com

 is a trademark of The 10 Books

Associate Publisher: Kim Koh
Project Editor: Amy Land
Editor: Joyce Thian
Project Manager/Designer: Jeanette MacLean
Graphic Designers: Rebecca Buchanan, Katherine Park

The publisher gratefully acknowledges the following for permission to reprint copyrighted material in this book.

Every reasonable effort has been made to trace the owners of copyrighted material and to make due acknowledgement. Any errors or omissions drawn to our attention will be gladly rectified in future editions.

"I Am Canadian" by Frank Misztal. From Peacekeeper's Home Page. Found at http://www.peacekeeper.ca/stories3.html

"World federation weighs in on hockey's origins" from CBC News, 5 July 2002. Courtesy of CBC.ca.

"Flag fliers 'proud of this country'" by Sandro Contenta. From *Toronto Star*, 30 June 2007. Reprinted with permission — Torstar Syndication Services.

Cover: Totem Pole–istockphoto; Rocky mountains–shutterstock

7 8 9 10 11   5 4 3 2 1

Library and Archives Canada Cataloguing in Publication

Dick, Karen
 The 10 most outstanding Canadian symbols/Karen Dick and Robert Cutting.

ISBN 978-1-55448-308-2

 1. Readers (Elementary) 2. Readers — Signs and symbols — Canada.
I. Cutting, Robert, 1952- II. Title. III. Title: Ten most outstanding Canadian symbols.

PE1117.D52 2007   428.6   C2007-903727-5

Contents

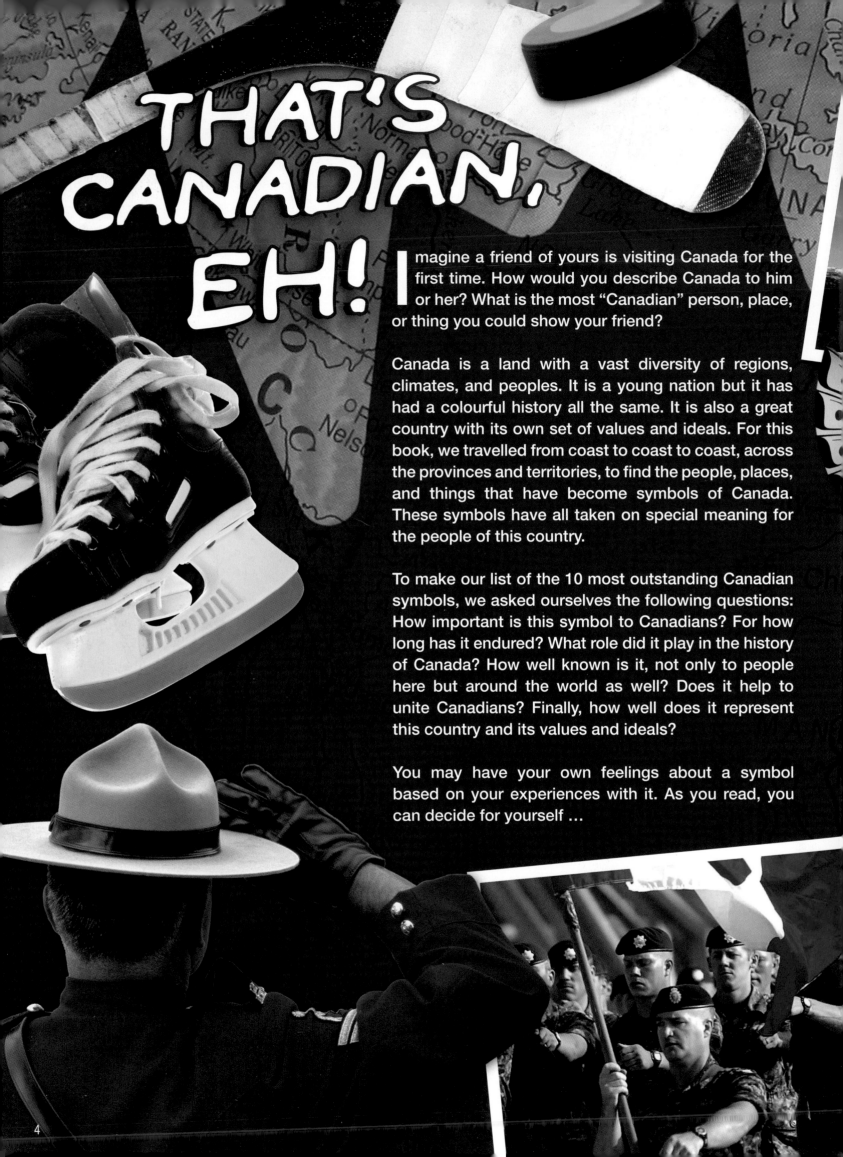

THAT'S CANADIAN, EH!

Imagine a friend of yours is visiting Canada for the first time. How would you describe Canada to him or her? What is the most "Canadian" person, place, or thing you could show your friend?

Canada is a land with a vast diversity of regions, climates, and peoples. It is a young nation but it has had a colourful history all the same. It is also a great country with its own set of values and ideals. For this book, we travelled from coast to coast to coast, across the provinces and territories, to find the people, places, and things that have become symbols of Canada. These symbols have all taken on special meaning for the people of this country.

To make our list of the 10 most outstanding Canadian symbols, we asked ourselves the following questions: How important is this symbol to Canadians? For how long has it endured? What role did it play in the history of Canada? How well known is it, not only to people here but around the world as well? Does it help to unite Canadians? Finally, how well does it represent this country and its values and ideals?

You may have your own feelings about a symbol based on your experiences with it. As you read, you can decide for yourself ...

WHAT IS THE MOST OUTSTANDING CANADIAN SYMBOL?

Anne of Green Gables *has been translated into 15 different languages and turned into a number of movies, television series, and plays.*

EN GABLES

WHAT IS IT? A fictional character created by author Lucy Maud Montgomery

WHAT IT REPRESENTS: Anne is an enduring example of imagination, optimism, and PEI charm.

It seems as if it was only yesterday that we were introduced to Anne Shirley of Avonlea. That would be Anne spelled with an "e"; Anne whose hair was as red as carrots; Anne of the picturesque Green Gables; Anne whose adventures have by now captured the hearts and minds of millions of readers.

Canada's own orphan Anne was created nearly 100 years ago by author Lucy Maud Montgomery of Prince Edward Island. People of all ages here in Canada and around the world continue to fall in love with one of the most enduring characters in literary history. Besides all the books and short stories Montgomery wrote about her, Anne is the star of numerous television shows, plays, musicals, and even movies.

The heartwarming tales of Anne and her life growing up on the East Coast are an important part of Canada's cultural heritage. The plucky orphan from PEI takes the #10 spot on our list of the most outstanding Canadian symbols.

---

heritage: *things that have been passed down from earlier generations*

ANNE OF GREEN GABLES

BACKGROUND

Anne made her debut in *Anne of Green Gables*, published in 1908. The book was an instant success. Though written for younger readers, it appealed to a much wider audience. Author Lucy Maud Montgomery wrote seven sequels about Anne's teaching career, marriage to Gilbert Blythe, and their family: *Anne of Avonlea* (1909), *Anne of the Island* (1915), *Anne's House of Dreams* (1917), *Rainbow Valley* (1919), *Rilla of Ingleside* (1921), *Anne of Windy Poplars* (1936), and *Anne of Ingleside* (1939).

> **?** Anne's character aged and matured at practically the same speed as her readers. Do you think this is a good technique for writers to use? Why or why not?

ANALYZE THIS!

The character of Anne is full of life and energy. She's bright and adventurous, loyal and unapologetic, talkative and imaginative. She's also stubbornly optimistic, despite her tragic past. Besides her infectious personality, Anne is also remembered for her love of and respect for nature. She spends a lot of time outdoors and gives adoring names to the beautiful surroundings of her rural PEI community.

IT'S OFFICIAL

Shortly after Montgomery passed away, the Historic Sites and Monuments Board of Canada officially recognized her as a "person of national historic significance." It put a monument and plaque at the real-life Green Gables in Cavendish, PEI. The farmhouse and surrounding area were designated as an official National Historic Site. From 1993 to 1997, PEI issued licence plates with the slogan "Home of Anne of Green Gables" and an image of Anne.

Quick Fact

Most of the places in Anne's fictional hometown of Avonlea were based on real places in the small rural community of Cavendish, PEI.

The Expert Says...

" The freckle-faced, red-haired and verbosely romantic orphan dream, Anne Shirley, has become the closest any Canadian literary equivalent can get to Mickey Mouse. "

— Geoff Pevere and Greig Dymond in *Mondo Canuck: A Canadian Pop Culture Odyssey*

verbosely: *being too wordy*

The Anne doll is a popular item at the Anne of Green Gables Store in Cavendish, PEI.

Quick Fact

American writer Mark Twain once wrote a letter to Lucy Maud Montgomery to compliment her on her work. He called Anne the "most lovable childhood heroine since the immortal Alice."

Searching for Green Gables

The Green Gables farmhouse was designated as a National Historic Site for its importance in Canadian literary history.

More than 50 million copies of Lucy Maud Montgomery's first book about Anne have been sold worldwide. Check out this report to see how this popular Canadian novel has attracted tourists to PEI through the years!

In the first five months after it was published, 19 000 copies of *Anne of Green Gables* were sold. *Anne* went into 10 printings in its first year. By the following year, it was being translated so that more people worldwide could read her story.

With *Anne* proving so popular, what came next should not have surprised anyone in PEI. Flocks of the book's fans soon began to arrive on the Island. They wanted to see the "real" Avonlea.

Anne fans came from all around the world, including the United States, England, China, and Japan. Everyone wanted a piece of the "situation and scenery" that Montgomery said had inspired her to create the beautiful setting in her book.

From Lover's Lane to Haunted Wood to Green Gables, it could all be found in Cavendish, PEI, where Montgomery grew up. As the government of PEI proudly proclaims, *Anne* was "inspired by the land, the sea, and the people around her. It in turn has imparted an image of the Island that draws 350 000 visitors annually from around the world … ."

Take Note

Anne of Green Gables kicks off our list of the 10 most outstanding Canadian symbols. She is a world-famous character with strong Canadian roots. She is a huge part of this country's cultural heritage and continues to promote PEI and Canada to international audiences.
- It has been nearly 100 years since Anne was created. Why do you think today's readers still connect to her character and story?

? If you were to write a fictional story, how could you use your own surroundings and community for inspiration?

5   4   3   2   1

Bluenose was named "Queen of the North Atlantic Fishing Fleet" because of its outstanding performance on the seas.

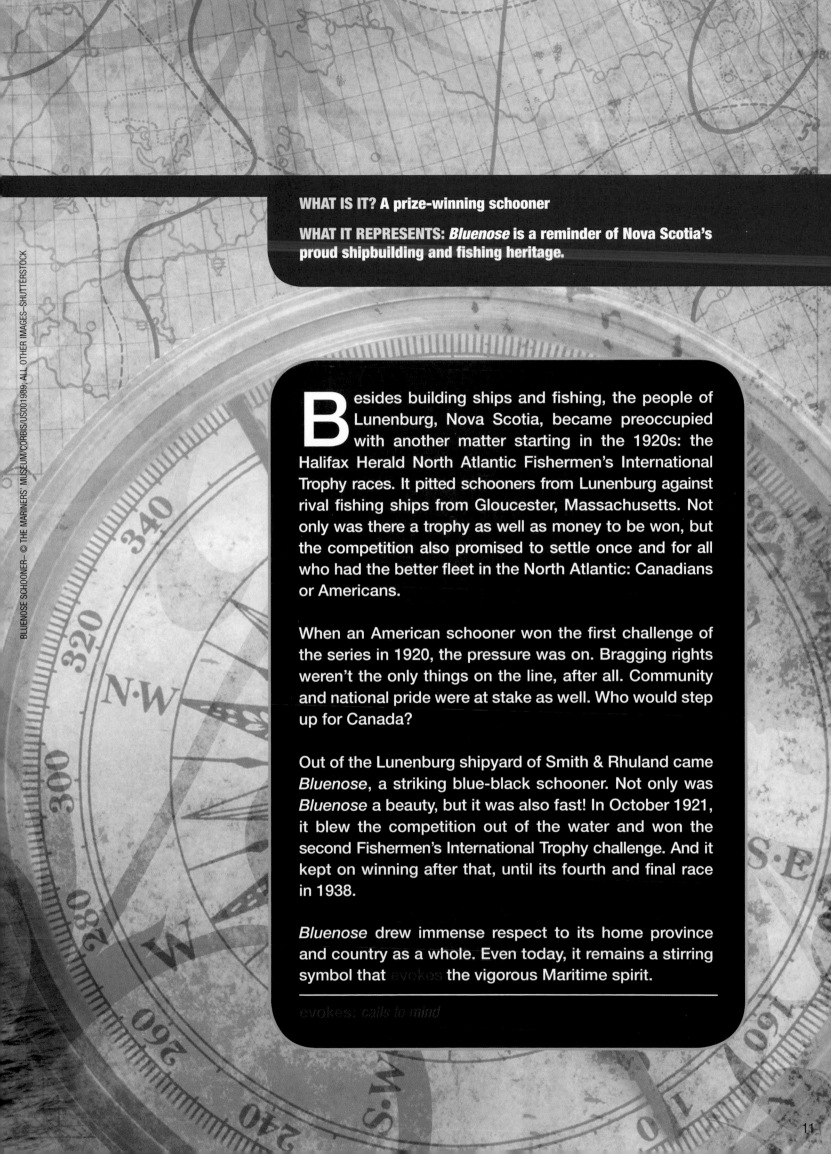

WHAT IS IT? A prize-winning schooner

WHAT IT REPRESENTS: *Bluenose* is a reminder of Nova Scotia's proud shipbuilding and fishing heritage.

Besides building ships and fishing, the people of Lunenburg, Nova Scotia, became preoccupied with another matter starting in the 1920s: the Halifax Herald North Atlantic Fishermen's International Trophy races. It pitted schooners from Lunenburg against rival fishing ships from Gloucester, Massachusetts. Not only was there a trophy as well as money to be won, but the competition also promised to settle once and for all who had the better fleet in the North Atlantic: Canadians or Americans.

When an American schooner won the first challenge of the series in 1920, the pressure was on. Bragging rights weren't the only things on the line, after all. Community and national pride were at stake as well. Who would step up for Canada?

Out of the Lunenburg shipyard of Smith & Rhuland came *Bluenose*, a striking blue-black schooner. Not only was *Bluenose* a beauty, but it was also fast! In October 1921, it blew the competition out of the water and won the second Fishermen's International Trophy challenge. And it kept on winning after that, until its fourth and final race in 1938.

Bluenose drew immense respect to its home province and country as a whole. Even today, it remains a stirring symbol that evokes the vigorous Maritime spirit.

evokes: calls to mind

11

BLUENOSE

BACKGROUND

Bluenose was first and foremost a fishing schooner. Besides having an unbeaten record in the Fishermen's International Trophy races, *Bluenose* also landed record hauls of cod. At the height of its racing career, *Bluenose* was chosen twice to represent Canada on the world stage. In 1933, it was at the "Century of Progress" World's Fair in Chicago. Two years after that, it sailed to England for the celebration of the 25th year of King George V's reign.

IT'S OFFICIAL

In 1929, Canada Post celebrated *Bluenose*'s impressive victories by issuing a special stamp called the "Fifty-cent *Bluenose* Commemorative." In 1937, an image of *Bluenose* was chosen as the face of the new Canadian dime. Since 1989, Nova Scotia has been issuing licence plates with an image of *Bluenose* in the background.

In the 1920s, Lunenburg was a booming port and boasted the finest fishing fleets in the world.

ANALYZE THIS!

Bluenose's grace and superior sailing abilities were attributed to the superb work of Nova Scotia shipwrights. In those days, the fishing and shipbuilding industries were a huge part of life on the East Coast. *Bluenose* was also seen as extremely tough and dependable. It lasted nearly 20 seasons on the seas, while the average lifespan for a fishing boat at the time was around 10 years.

shipwrights: *carpenters who build or repair ships*

The Expert Says...

"People from all walks of life and from ports all over the world still respond to the romantic past which *Bluenose II* suggests. Millions of people have boarded her, sailed on her, or simply looked at her ... ."

— Cheryl Sullivan, journalist, *Nova Scotia Historical Review*

Quick Fact

As soon as advertisers realized how famous *Bluenose* was becoming, they began to use its name and image to sell all sorts of products, including calendars, milk, paint, tea, skis, and even underwear!

? Do you think it was appropriate for advertisers to use a national symbol like *Bluenose* to sell their products? Why or why not?

Bluenose By the Numbers

97 — number of days it took to build *Bluenose* by hand

26.21 km/h — *Bluenose*'s average speed during its final race. This still stands as the fastest pace ever recorded by a canvassed vessel over a fixed course.

293 020 kg — weight of *Bluenose*'s record haul of Atlantic cod in 1923

1946 — the year *Bluenose* reportedly ran onto a reef near Haiti. It sank to the bottom and was never retrieved.

1955 — the year *Bluenose* and her captain, Angus Walters, were inducted into Canada's Sports Hall of Fame. It was the Hall's first non-human inductee.

1963 — the year *Bluenose II* made its debut

$35,000 — total cost to build *Bluenose* in 1921

$300,000 — total cost to build *Bluenose II* in 1963

Bluenose II was built from the same plans and in the same shipyard as the original Bluenose.

Quick Fact

Bluenose II is an important tourist attraction in Nova Scotia. It routinely sails to other ports on the East Coast of Canada and the United States to help promote the province.

Take Note

Like Anne at #10, *Bluenose* is an important part of Canadian heritage. But *Bluenose* ranks higher on our list, because it evokes a proud time in Maritime history when Nova Scotia was at the top of its form in fishing, shipbuilding, and seafaring.

• What is your home province best known for? How could you promote this aspect of your province to the rest of Canada and the world?

10 CENTS

(8) INUKSUK

The inuksuk seen here was built to welcome tourists to the resort town of Whistler, BC.

WHAT IS IT? A stack of rocks piled into any form or size that can serve many different purposes

WHAT IT REPRESENTS: The inuksuk is a symbol of the strength and inventiveness of the Inuit peoples of Canada.

To most people, the northern regions of Canada can seem pretty desolate. But the Inuit have been living there for many generations. How were they able to find their way around and survive in such a vast landscape?

The solution was simple yet brilliant. The Inuit began to make markers out of rocks, piling them into stacks of various forms and sizes. They called these *inuksuit* (plural for *inuksuk*). *Inuk* meaning human and *suk* meaning substitute, the inuksuk became a central part of navigation in the North. It was an ingenious way of passing on all sorts of important information that was critical to survival.

Today, the inuksuk is a common feature of the landscape in northern Canada. The Inuit continue the tradition of building inuksuit, some for many new purposes nowadays. Distinct and unique to the land, the inuksuk stands at #8.

INUKSUK

BACKGROUND

The Inuit build different-looking inuksuit to serve a variety of purposes. Some act as a sign of welcome at the entrance to a home or community. Some point travellers in the right direction. Some help indicate a good hunting, fishing, or gathering spot. Some stand guard as a warning of possible danger. Some physically help hunters round up prey. Built with rocks and piled by experienced hands, an inuksuk can last hundreds of years in the harsh conditions of the North.

ANALYZE THIS!

The inuksuk was a simple and effective way of communicating with and helping others — no modern technology needed. It's a great illustration of the spirit of the Inuit, who have now lived and flourished in one of the world's harshest landscapes for many hundreds of years. The sturdy and helpful inuksuk conveys strength and persistence, as well as friendship and leadership. Built with pieces of the earth, the inuksuk is also a symbol of the Inuit peoples' connection and harmony with nature and the land.

IT'S OFFICIAL

An image of an inuksuk was chosen for the flags of two regions in Canada populated by Inuit: Nunavut, the new territory created in 1999, and Nunatsiavut, the regional Inuit government in Newfoundland and Labrador, formed in 2005. An inuksuk shaped like a human (called an *inunnguaq*) is being used as the symbol of the Vancouver 2010 Olympic Games.

> Some people have said that the Vancouver Olympic committee's use of an *inunnguaq* is inappropriate. Do some research on the arguments for and against the use of the symbol. Where do you stand on the issue?

The Expert Says...

" This intriguing Inuit cultural symbol honours a vital part of what constitutes Canadian identity — the North and the impact of Inuit culture on Canada's national identity. "

— Nadine Fabbi, associate director, Canadian Studies Center, University of Washington

Quick Fact

Historians aren't completely sure when the Inuit started making and using inuksuit in northern Canada. Most believe the practice began as soon as they migrated here from Alaska, between 1000 and 1200 CE.

10   8   7   6

LAND OF THE INUKSUK

Check out this photo essay for a glimpse of just some of the many different forms of inuksuk that can be found all over northern Canada. You'll see that no two inuksuit look the same or even serve the same purpose …

An inuksuk placed near a lake might show that fish can be found in the lake at the same distance the figure is placed from the shoreline.

Travellers out in open land welcome the sight of a familiar-looking inuksuk. It tells them exactly where they are and which way they should go next.

An inuksuk with two legs found near water or a coastline may point to an open channel for navigation.

A row of inuksuit helps to corral caribou along a path and direct them toward waiting hunters.

An inuksuk can be used as a symbol of respect if erected as a memorial.

A modern-day inuksuk might be placed in a garden or picnic spot to signify peace and beauty.

Quick Fact

According to Inuit tradition, inuksuit are sacred and should never be destroyed.

Take Note

The inuksuk comes in at #8. Still standing tall and proud after so many years, inuksuit are reminders of the Inuit peoples' toughness and spirit, their remarkable culture, and their ability to survive in and make the most of Canada's harshest landscape.
• Imagine building an inuksuk in your community with the help of an Inuit artist. What would be the purpose of your inuksuk? Where would you put it and how would you shape it?

5   4   3   2   1

In July 2003, Canadian soldiers took command of the international peacekeeping force in Afghanistan. The peacekeepers were there to help maintain security in the capital city, Kabul.

ING

WHAT IS IT? Placing neutral forces in the middle of a conflict to stop and prevent violence between opposing groups

WHAT IT REPRESENTS: Canada's commitment to peace and non-violence

A round the world, peacekeepers risk their lives to help people they have never met. They risk their lives to bring peace to countries they have likely never been to. They risk their lives in hopes of making this world a safe place for you and me to live in.

There's no doubt that being a peacekeeper is a dangerous job. But it's something that countless Canadians have done without hesitation. And they've done it with absolute pride, too. This should come as no surprise. Canada was one of the first countries in the world to officially commit itself to peace as part of its defence policy.

An influential symbol of Canada's commitment to making peace, not war, peacekeeping comes in at #7 on our list.

PEACEKEEPERS—AAP IMAGES/XINHUA/WANG LEE

PEACEKEEPING

BACKGROUND

In 1956, there were signs that a conflict in the Middle East could turn into a global war. Anxious to prevent World War III, the United Nations (UN) sent in the world's first peacekeeping force. Made up of soldiers from neutral countries, the job of the force was to stop the fighting, separate the warring armies, and ease the conflict. This groundbreaking idea came from Canada's then foreign minister, Lester B. Pearson. The force was first led by a Canadian soldier.

? Some people argue that Canada should focus on domestic security instead of international peacekeeping. What do you think?

ANALYZE THIS!

Peacekeeping is a tough, selfless, and noble way of ensuring peace and security in the world. Instead of starting wars, peacekeepers do their best to stop them. Many see peacekeeping as the perfect and most valuable role for Canada to take in the global community. It goes with Canada's "unmilitary" reputation.

? After decades of never refusing, Canada no longer accepts every peacekeeping mission established by the UN. Do you think this will hurt Canada's reputation abroad? Why or why not?

IT'S OFFICIAL

For helping to create the world's first peacekeeping force, Lester B. Pearson got the Nobel Peace Prize in 1957. Peacekeeping soon became a part of Canada's official foreign policy in the postwar period. In 1988, the Canadian Peacekeeping Service Medal was created to honour peacekeepers who have made a unique contribution to peace. In 1992, the National Peacekeeping Monument was built in Ottawa. Two years after that, the government established the Lester B. Pearson Canadian International Peacekeeping Training Centre on an old military base in Clementsport, Nova Scotia.

foreign policy: *policy in interacting with other nations*

Located in Ottawa, the Peacekeeping Monument, entitled Reconciliation, *is the only monument of its kind in the world.*

The Expert Says...

" For nearly half a century, peacekeeping has been the core of our foreign policy and the fabric of our national identity. We have prided ourselves on being a global mediator, a reputation that has earned us respect worldwide. "

— Craig and Marc Kielburger, activists and founders of Free the Children

10 9 8 7 6

I Am ❤ Canadian

Check out this list written by retired peacekeeper Master Corporal Frank Misztal!

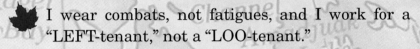🍁 I wear combats, not fatigues, and I work for a "LEFT-tenant," not a "LOO-tenant."

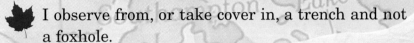🍁 I observe from, or take cover in, a trench and not a foxhole.

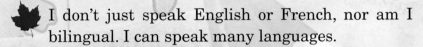🍁 I don't just speak English or French, nor am I bilingual. I can speak many languages.

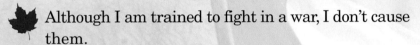🍁 Although I am trained to fight in a war, I don't cause them.

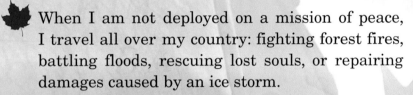🍁 When I am not deployed on a mission of peace, I travel all over my country: fighting forest fires, battling floods, rescuing lost souls, or repairing damages caused by an ice storm.

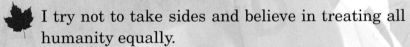🍁 I try not to take sides and believe in treating all humanity equally.

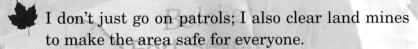🍁 I don't just go on patrols; I also clear land mines to make the area safe for everyone.

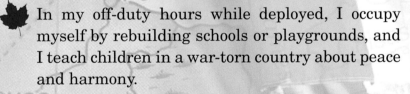🍁 In my off-duty hours while deployed, I occupy myself by rebuilding schools or playgrounds, and I teach children in a war-torn country about peace and harmony.

🍁 I am my country's best ambassador and I am respected the world over for what I do best.

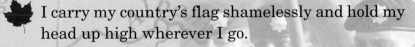🍁 I carry my country's flag shamelessly and hold my head up high wherever I go.

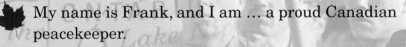🍁 My name is Frank, and I am … a proud Canadian peacekeeper.

Quick Fact

Peacekeepers don't just keep the peace. They also help civilians affected by a conflict. They deliver food and medicine, clear land mines, and rebuild basic facilities, such as roads, bridges, water pipes, and power lines.

Take Note

When Canadian peacekeepers go out into the world, they are working to achieve peace via the most non-violent route possible. Canadians across the country couldn't be prouder of their military's ability and willingness to play such a valuable role on the world stage. Peacekeeping comes in at #7 on our list.
• Do you think you could be a peacekeeper? What qualities does such work require?

6 TOTEM POLE

Stanley Park in Vancouver, BC, features a number of authentic totem poles carved by different First Nations artists from the West Coast.

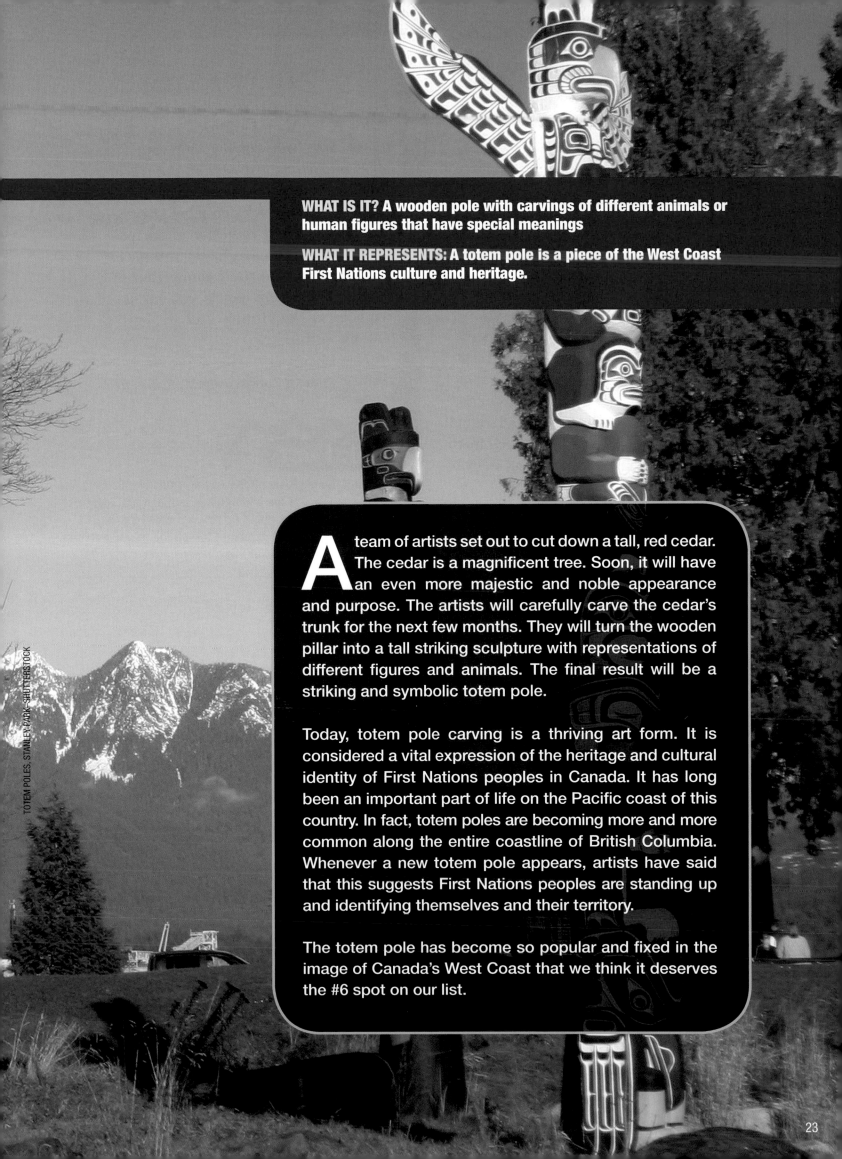

WHAT IS IT? A wooden pole with carvings of different animals or human figures that have special meanings

WHAT IT REPRESENTS: A totem pole is a piece of the West Coast First Nations culture and heritage.

A team of artists set out to cut down a tall, red cedar. The cedar is a magnificent tree. Soon, it will have an even more majestic and noble appearance and purpose. The artists will carefully carve the cedar's trunk for the next few months. They will turn the wooden pillar into a tall striking sculpture with representations of different figures and animals. The final result will be a striking and symbolic totem pole.

Today, totem pole carving is a thriving art form. It is considered a vital expression of the heritage and cultural identity of First Nations peoples in Canada. It has long been an important part of life on the Pacific coast of this country. In fact, totem poles are becoming more and more common along the entire coastline of British Columbia. Whenever a new totem pole appears, artists have said that this suggests First Nations peoples are standing up and identifying themselves and their territory.

The totem pole has become so popular and fixed in the image of Canada's West Coast that we think it deserves the #6 spot on our list.

TOTEM POLE

BACKGROUND

The Haida, Tlingit, and Tsimshian peoples on the Pacific coast were the first to carve tall totem poles with multiple figures. Soon, poles appeared all along the coast as more First Nations people took up the art form. This didn't last. By the late 1800s, as Canadian society changed, the number of totem poles being made dropped. It wasn't until the late 1950s that a new generation of First Nations artists from the West Coast revived the totem pole. They relearned their histories and languages and used their art to assert their political identities and rights in a new Canada. Old poles were reclaimed and restored; new poles were carved in even greater numbers than ever before.

ANALYZE THIS!

Totem poles have artistic and historical value. Through different figures and features, a totem pole can convey different messages. Most importantly, it says to the world exactly who its owners are, where they're from, what they've experienced, and what they believe in. The striking and majestic totem pole shows First Nations people's pride in their identities and histories, and their connection to nature. Finally, the totem pole's revival is seen as symbolic of the vitality and strength of First Nations culture.

vitality: *power to survive; capacity to live, grow, or develop*

Quick Fact

As First Nations artists on the Pacific coast stopped making new totem poles in the late 1800s, European and American museums started snapping up finished poles for their collections. Increasing exposure turned the totem pole into an international symbol of First Nations culture.

IT'S OFFICIAL

Totem poles made by West Coast artists have been installed in a number of Canadian embassies abroad. In 1981, the United Nations designated SGang Gwaay, an old Haida village on Anthony Island of the Queen Charlotte Islands, British Columbia, as a World Heritage site. Some of the world's oldest totem poles stand there.

"Low on the totem pole" is a common saying that means you're the least important person in an organization. However, when it comes to actual totem poles, the lowest figures are in fact often the most important!

6

GET IT RIGHT!

Check out this list of some of the most popular (but incorrect) myths about totem poles and see if you can separate fact from fiction!

MYTH > Totem poles were used for worship or for warding off evil spirits.

FACT >> Totem poles have never served either of these purposes! They've always simply acted as emblems or reminders of a family or clan and its history.

MYTH > You can read a totem pole like a book.

FACT >> Sure, you could guess at what the figures on a pole might be. However, it's not possible to know what the pole really means without knowing the history of the pole, its creator, or the family or clan that owns it.

MYTH > Carvings on totem poles are always very serious.

FACT >> Actually, carvers have often added little touches of humour into their poles. Sometimes, figures are "accidentally" carved upside down. Or, a little winking or grinning figure might peek out from behind a bigger figure.

MYTH > Totem poles last thousands of years.

FACT >> Even though most totem poles are made of decay-resistant cedar, they will still fall over in about 100 years. However, the First Nations on the Pacific coast have a tradition of carving identical copies of fallen poles. The new poles are then raised by the descendants of the original pole's owners.

The Expert Says...

"Totem poles should be treated as beautiful objects of contemplation as well as artifacts that inform or educate us about the past. ... These massive carvings represent a cultural tradition that flourished along our coastline for centuries ... ."

— Marjorie M. Halpin, anthropologist, author of *Totem Poles*

contemplation: *thoughtful observation or study*

? Many modern totem poles are carved by people with no connection to First Nations communities. Do you think it is appropriate for non-Aboriginal people to make totem poles? Why or why not?

Take Note

The totem pole is one of the most recognizable forms of Aboriginal art. Each comes with symbolic, cultural, and historical value. Considering its history and prevalence on the West Coast, the totem pole deserves the #6 spot on our list of the most outstanding Canadian symbols.

- If you were to make a sculpture to represent your cultural background, what figures or designs would you carve? Explain.

5   4   3   2   1

⑤ NIAGARA FAL

Niagara Falls gets more than 14 million visitors per year, which makes it one of the most popular tourist attractions in North America.

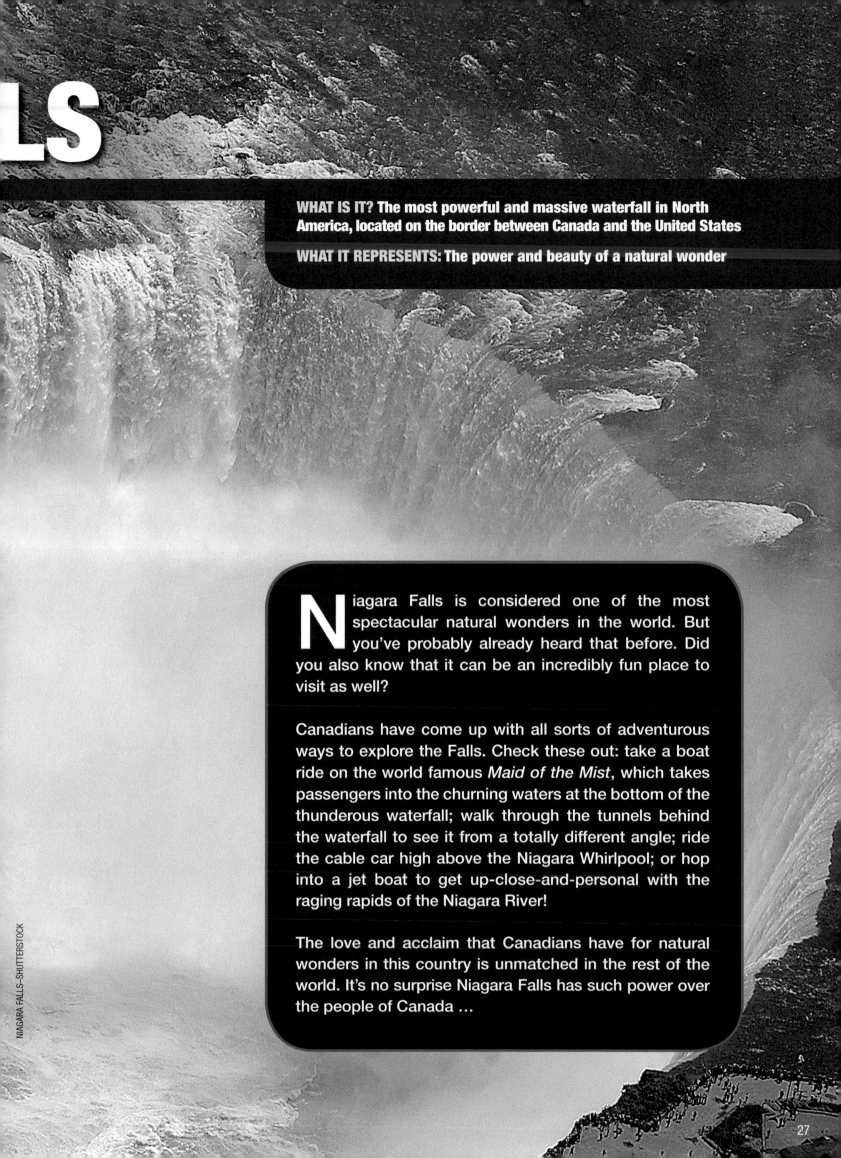

LS

WHAT IS IT? The most powerful and massive waterfall in North America, located on the border between Canada and the United States

WHAT IT REPRESENTS: The power and beauty of a natural wonder

Niagara Falls is considered one of the most spectacular natural wonders in the world. But you've probably already heard that before. Did you also know that it can be an incredibly fun place to visit as well?

Canadians have come up with all sorts of adventurous ways to explore the Falls. Check these out: take a boat ride on the world famous *Maid of the Mist*, which takes passengers into the churning waters at the bottom of the thunderous waterfall; walk through the tunnels behind the waterfall to see it from a totally different angle; ride the cable car high above the Niagara Whirlpool; or hop into a jet boat to get up-close-and-personal with the raging rapids of the Niagara River!

The love and acclaim that Canadians have for natural wonders in this country is unmatched in the rest of the world. It's no surprise Niagara Falls has such power over the people of Canada ...

NIAGARA FALLS–SHUTTERSTOCK

NIAGARA FALLS

BACKGROUND

Formed about 10 000 to 12 000 years ago, Niagara Falls is a set of three waterfalls. It's located at around the halfway point of the Niagara River, which separates Canada and the United States. Where the river becomes divided by Goat Island, 90 percent of it flows to the horseshoe-shaped Canadian Falls (named Horseshoe Falls), while the rest flows to the American Falls. At the American Falls, another small island further splits the river to create a third, small waterfall (named Bridal Veil Falls). Of the three, Horseshoe Falls is the most massive and powerful. It spans 670 metres across, and has a drop of about 56 metres.

Quick Fact

The rushing waters of Niagara Falls serve as one of the world's greatest sources of hydroelectric power. Power plants on both the Canadian and American sides of the Falls harness enough power to produce nearly 4.5 million kilowatts of electricity.

ANALYZE THIS!

Niagara Falls is a natural wonder that many consider breathtaking and awe-inspiring. In the past, the Falls' raging and crushing waters seemed dangerous, too powerful, and untameable. But now, the Falls seem to have more of a romantic appeal. The city of Niagara Falls has become the wedding capital of Canada!

IT'S OFFICIAL

The Ontario government passed the Niagara Falls Park Act on 30 March 1885. This led to the creation of the Niagara Falls Park Commission, which became responsible for preserving and enhancing the natural beauty of Niagara Falls, the Niagara Gorge, and the Niagara River.

 Do some more research on Niagara Falls. Why is it considered a geological wonder?

The Expert Says...

“ The Falls is among the most documented, filmed, and painted sites in the world … . It has inspired genius, greed, fear, affection, virtue, romance, and passion. ”

— John Grant, executive producer of the PBS show *Niagara Falls*

Taking the PLUNGE

Many adventure-seekers have been lured to Niagara Falls. Seeking fame or fortune, they try to cross the waterfall on a tightrope, go over it in a barrel, or shoot the rapids below. As of 2004, 16 daredevils have made documented trips over the Falls. Eleven have survived. Check out the list below for the first three successful daredevils to have survived a plunge!

1. ANNIE TAYLOR, 24 OCTOBER 1901
- A retired school teacher from Bay City, Michigan
- The first person to go over the Falls — took the plunge in a wooden barrel
- Suffered gashes and a concussion and said afterwards, "Nobody ought ever to do that again."

2. BOBBY LEACH, 25 JULY 1911
- A circus stuntman from Cornwall, England
- The first man to go over the Falls — took the plunge in a steel barrel
- Broke his jaw and both kneecaps

3. JEAN LUSSIER, 4 JULY 1928
- A machinist from Springfield, Massachusetts, who grew up in Quebec
- Took the plunge in a large rubber ball that was covered with steel bands and lined with inner tubes that acted as shock absorbers
- The ball's outer and inner linings were both heavily damaged, but Lussier himself emerged relatively unscathed.

unscathed: not injured or harmed

Quick Fact
Niagara Falls shocked visitors and locals when it stopped flowing on 29 March 1848. An ice jam at the mouth of the Niagara River reduced the water flow to a trickle for 30 to 40 hours.

Take Note
Niagara Falls is one spectacular sight! Millions of people come to Canada to visit the Falls every year — no other place in Canada is as famous or recognized internationally. The Falls' power, both in helping to produce electricity and inspiring awe in Canada's beautiful environment, earns it the #5 spot on our list.
- There are numerous other natural wonders across Canada, such as the Rocky Mountains and the Bay of Fundy. What makes the Falls more iconic than these other sites?

? Why do you think someone who considers himself or herself a "stunt person" or "daredevil" would want to take on the challenge of going over Niagara Falls?

5   4   3   2   1

④ BEAVER

The beaver is called a rodent because it is a mammal with large front teeth that it uses for gnawing.

WHAT IS IT? A brown, buck-toothed rodent

WHAT IT REPRESENTS: The quiet, unassuming, and hardworking nature of the people of Canada

Who would have thought that a rodent could mean so much to a country? To be fair, the furry brown beaver is one of the most adorable rodents around. And, of course, it played a huge role in this country's early history and development!

Aboriginal people in Canada were the first to recognize the value of the beaver. They hunted it, roasting the meat for food and using the pelts for clothing. With the arrival of the first Europeans, the furry animal soon became a prized commodity. In the 16th century, explorers from Europe began exchanging metal and cloth goods for the beaver's thick furs. When they returned home, they made lots of money selling the furs. Turns out beaver pelt made great hats! By the end of the century, beaver hats had become the biggest fashion trend of the day. Demand for beaver pelts soared. More and more European explorers and fur traders came to Canada looking for beaver furs. And the rest, as they say, was history.

Turn the page to read more about the beaver and its journey to becoming one of the most outstanding Canadian symbols.

---

commodity: *valuable good; item that is traded*

BEAVER

BACKGROUND

The North American beaver can be found throughout Canada, all the way north to the mouths of the Mackenzie and Coppermine Rivers on the Arctic Ocean. The huge demand in Europe for beaver pelt from the late 1600s all the way until the 1830s resulted in two major developments here in Canada. It led France and England to establish settlements and trading posts to engage in the fur trade. It kick-started their exploration, mapping, and fight over these lands, from the Maritimes to the Pacific and Arctic Oceans.

ANALYZE THIS!

Besides human beings, the beaver does more to shape its landscape than any other mammal on Earth. The beaver is a hard-working and productive creature. Even when it was being hunted to near extinction in Canada at one time, it survived, by moving westward. The beaver has come to symbolize diligence, perseverance, and determination.

Quick Fact

Many people admire the beaver for being nature's engineer. A number of schools have adopted the beaver as their mascots, including the Massachusetts Institute of Technology, California Institute of Technology, Oregon State University, and University of Toronto.

IT'S OFFICIAL

In 1673, the governor general suggested to the royal authorities that the beaver be made the symbol for young Canada, because he knew how important the trade in beaver pelts was in this country. The first Canadian postage stamp was the "Three Penny Beaver," introduced in 1851. Then, in 1975, via the National Symbol of Canada Act, the beaver attained official status as an emblem of Canada. In the 1976 Olympics, Montreal chose "Amik" the beaver as the Games' official mascot.

Canada isn't the only country to have a national animal. Other well-known national animals include the giant panda (China), Bengal tiger (India), bear (Russia), bull (Spain), and bald eagle (United States). How would you compare the beaver to any one of these national animals?

The Expert Says...

No other animal has influenced Canada's history to the extent that the beaver has. When Europeans began to settle in northern North America, beaver pelts were the prize that lured them farther and farther into the wilderness.

— Hinterland Who's Who website, Environment Canada

Beaver Bites

Check out this fact chart for three bites of information about Canada's celebrated beaver ...

1 The beaver's ancestor from prehistoric times was huge! The Giant Beaver of North America measured up to 2.5 m long (the size of a black bear) and weighed about 220 kg (seven times the size of the modern beaver). It became extinct during the Ice Age, about 10 000 years ago. Fossils of the Giant Beaver have been found in Toronto and the Old Crow region of the Yukon.

2 The pelt of North American beavers became a hot commodity in the 1600s, because the Europeans had already wiped out their own beaver populations. At that time the water-repellent beaver hat was fashionable and also very useful in rainy England. The umbrella had not yet been invented.

3 A number of superstitions used to surround the beaver. It was said that wearing a beaver fur hat could make you smarter or even cure deafness! Rubbing oil produced by a beaver into the hair was even supposed to improve memory.

Quick Fact
A group of Canadian engineers have celebrated the last Friday in February as "National Beaver Day" every year since 1974!

Take Note
The admirable beaver takes the #4 spot on our list, because it played a big role in the founding of Canada. The fur trade greatly shaped the early history of this country, encouraging and influencing new settlements and explorations.
- Some people say the beaver is a "weak" and even "insignificant" animal. How would you explain to them the value and meaning behind the beaver?

5   **4**   3   2   1

The Mounties may be Canada's best-known symbol internationally, and you can bet it has a lot to do with their distinctive ceremonial uniform.

Besides a Mountie, who else could wear a wide-brimmed hat, a red jacket, black riding pants, and brown leather boots and still command respect? Though they don't wear such a fancy outfit while on the job nowadays, Mounties still wear the "Red Serge" at special ceremonies and celebrations. It's pretty much the same uniform they've been wearing since the Mounted Police force was created more than 130 years ago. Talk about a blast from the past!

Beyond merely making a unique fashion statement, the Mounties show the rest of the world the Canadian way of maintaining law and order across a nation. They're one of Canada's most enduring and respected institutions. And as the national police force, they're a powerful symbol of Canadian identity from coast to coast. Helping keep the "True North strong and free," these noble figures are directly connected to the idea of peace and order in Canadian society.

Read on to find out more about the history and symbolic value of the Mounties, #3 on our list of the most outstanding Canadian symbols.

institutions: *organizations dedicated to public service*

RCMP ON HORSEBACK—© PAUL A. SOUDERS/CORBIS/SC004849

35

MOUNTIES

BACKGROUND

The RCMP started out as the North-West Mounted Police (NWMP). It was created in 1873 as a temporary police force to establish law and order on Canada's western frontiers. With the Prairies under control, the force expanded north in the late 1890s to help police the Klondike gold rush in the Yukon. In 1920, the government decided Canada needed a federal police force spread throughout the country. So, the NWMP absorbed the Dominion Police in the east and set up headquarters in Ottawa. In keeping with its new and expanded role, the force was renamed the Royal Canadian Mounted Police.

ANALYZE THIS!

The Mounties built a legendary reputation for bravery and persistence in the face of lawlessness. But, more importantly, they're also known and respected for balancing compassion with enforcement, which brings out a sense of pride and trust from Canadians. As for the Mounties' Red Serge uniform, historians say it will always evoke the "romance" and "adventure" of the great north.

IT'S OFFICIAL

In 1897, the NWMP represented Canada at a celebration for Queen Victoria in London. It also participated in the coronations of King Edward VII (1902) and King George V (1911). Today, at the international level, the RCMP acts as the Canadian representative of the International Criminal Police Organization (Interpol).

? Has the importance of the Mounties as a symbol of Canada increased or decreased over the years? Explain.

The RCMP says it strives to be a "progressive, proactive, and innovative" organization.

Quick Fact

Today, the RCMP handles federal policing, provincial policing (in all provinces except Ontario and Quebec), and municipal policing (in about 200 small communities). It also serves as the only police force in the Yukon, in Nunavut, and in the Northwest Territories.

The Expert Says...

" We're proud of our Mounties, known and respected throughout the world. When it comes to national symbols, there is simply nothing more potent, literally or figuratively more graphic. "

— Alan Kellogg, journalist, *Edmonton Journal*

potent: *powerful*

10   9   8   7   6

DRESSED FOR SUCCESS

Today, the Mounties save their Red Serge uniform for formal occasions such as civic ceremonies, public relations events, celebrations, and memorials. We break down the distinctive Mountie look in this labelled diagram:

STETSON: hat with a high crown, wide flat brim, and black band

TUNIC: red coat in military dress style, with low neck collar and brass buttons

BADGES: on the shoulders, collar, upper arms, and sleeves; badges can be for service, qualifications, and/or appointment

SAM BROWNE BELT: a black, specially designed belt with a cross strap; comes with a pistol holder, double magazine holder, and handcuff pouch

BREECHES: black riding pants with bulges at the hips and yellow striping down the outside of each leg

STRATHCONA BOOTS: brown leather riding boots (with attachable spurs)

Quick Fact

The Red Serge was passed down from the NWMP to today's RCMP. The original Mounted Police wore red jackets, because this set them apart from the Americans (who wore blue).

Take Note

The Mounties' day-to-day job and look may have changed since the 1870s, but they remain a proud and powerful symbol of peace and order in Canadian society. And they're still remembered for the role they played in Canada's early history. Recognized and respected around the world, the Mounties take the #3 spot on our list.

• If you worked for the RCMP, what would you do to help maintain its image so that Mounties remain a positive symbol of Canada?

5   4   **3**   2   1

Around 4.5 million people in Canada are involved in the sport of hockey — as coaches, players, officials, administrators, or volunteers.

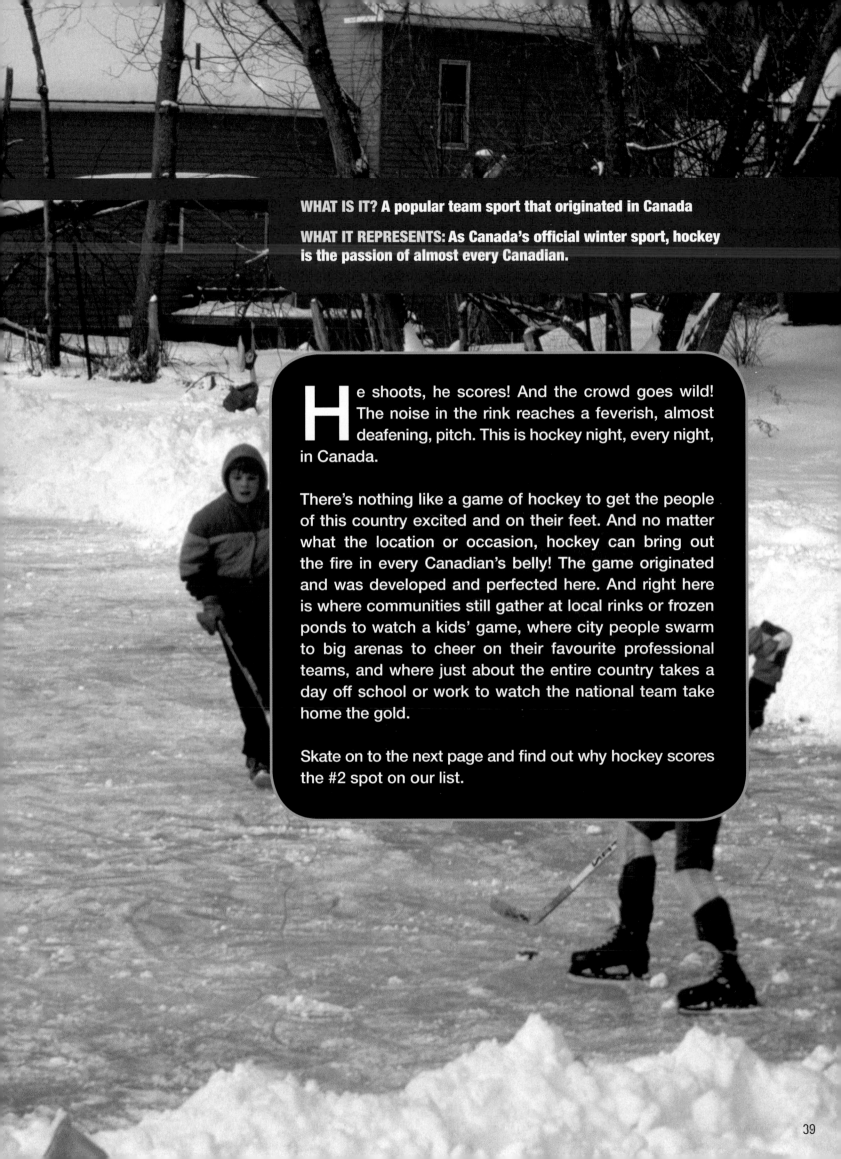

WHAT IS IT? A popular team sport that originated in Canada

WHAT IT REPRESENTS: As Canada's official winter sport, hockey is the passion of almost every Canadian.

He shoots, he scores! And the crowd goes wild! The noise in the rink reaches a feverish, almost deafening, pitch. This is hockey night, every night, in Canada.

There's nothing like a game of hockey to get the people of this country excited and on their feet. And no matter what the location or occasion, hockey can bring out the fire in every Canadian's belly! The game originated and was developed and perfected here. And right here is where communities still gather at local rinks or frozen ponds to watch a kids' game, where city people swarm to big arenas to cheer on their favourite professional teams, and where just about the entire country takes a day off school or work to watch the national team take home the gold.

Skate on to the next page and find out why hockey scores the #2 spot on our list.

HOCKEY

BACKGROUND

Though nobody knows for sure who invented this sport, historians believe the modern game of hockey was developed here in Canada. The first amateur hockey league was formed in Montreal in 1885. The game continues to evolve today and is now played by professionals and amateurs around the world. But Canada remains home to the greatest number of active hockey players.

Quick Fact

In 1917 several Canadian hockey teams banded together and founded the National Hockey League (NHL).

In 2006, the Canadian women's hockey team won its second straight Olympic gold medal.

ANALYZE THIS!

Canadian hockey players and national teams have won all sorts of medals, championships, trophies, and awards over the years for being the best at this game. In fact, you could say Canada's reputation on the hockey rink is pure gold! But there's more to hockey than winning. It isn't just a game — hockey brings Canadians together and keeps participants active and healthy. It's a sport that embodies the ideals of hard work, team effort, respect for others, and fair play. In 2003, a survey found that an increasing number of Canadians consider hockey a "very important" part of patriotism and Canada's national identity.

IT'S OFFICIAL

In 1994, the government created Hockey Canada, an organization whose goal was to develop, promote, manage, and run the national team that represents Canada in international hockey competition. Hockey Canada's regional branches work to encourage the development of the sport in every Canadian province and territory. The National Sports of Canada Act (1994) made hockey the country's official winter sport. In 2002, the Bank of Canada introduced a new $5 note featuring an image of children playing hockey.

? Do you like to play or watch hockey? What do you think appeals to hockey fans the most about the game?

The Expert Says...

" Hockey is also the history of Canadians. The game reflects the reality of Canada in its evolution, ambitions, character, tensions, and partnerships. "

— Roch Carrier, author of *Le chandail de hockey* (The Hockey Sweater)

10   9   8   7

WORLD FEDERATION WEIGHS IN ON HOCKEY'S ORIGINS

An article from CBC News, 5 July 2002

The brouhaha over hockey's birthplace went into overtime Friday, as the International Ice Hockey Federation took sides.

The organization picked Montreal over other Canadian communities — including Kingston, Ontario, and the spot near Windsor, Nova Scotia, where many Nova Scotians feel the first game was played.

In June, the Society for International Hockey Research released an 18-page report concluding that the first match was played at the Victoria Skating Rink in downtown Montreal on 3 March 1875.

On Friday, the federation confirmed that it has accepted the findings. It wants to put a plaque or some other historical marker on the site — which is now a four-storey parking garage at the corner of Stanley and Drummond streets.

Although sports that resembled hockey may have been played in other places before 1875, the first actual game with a puck, nets, and a specific set of rules was in Montreal, according to the federation.

Diehard Montreal hockey fans celebrated Friday's announcement, and called for the old Victoria Rink to be rebuilt and turned into the permanent home of the Stanley Cup trophy.

? Why do you think there is such a debate over hockey's origins? Why might a community want the official title of being hockey's true birthplace?

Take Note

Hockey breaks away from the pack to take the #2 spot on our list of Canadian symbols. Its roots in Canada, its imprint on Canadian communities and culture, and its nationwide appeal combine to give it true iconic status.
• If someone said to you that hockey is "just a game," how would you respond?

5   4   3   **2**   1

MAPLE LEAF

Since the day it was raised, the maple leaf flag has been called a symbol of the nation's unity, representing all the citizens of Canada without distinction of race, language, belief, or opinion.

It might seem unthinkable now but Canada's red maple leaf flag once caused a huge national uproar. When the flag flap swept across the country, everyone got involved, from average citizens to politicians to the media.

For years after Confederation, Canada simply flew Britain's Union Jack as its national flag. By the mid-1920s, the government had decided it was time for a change. The country needed its own national flag — it needed a uniquely Canadian flag. For 40 years, people came up with all sorts of ideas for a new national flag. Finally, in October 1964, a flag committee narrowed thousands of designs down to three. The choices: a red flag with the Union Jack and the fleur-de-lis; a white flag with three red maple leaves in the centre and two blue bars on the sides; and finally a white flag with just a single red maple leaf in the centre and two red bars on the sides.

After much heated debate, voting finally took place in the wee hours of the morning of 15 December 1965. The simple red and white flag with a red maple leaf in the centre won! It was a symbolic victory for the maple leaf. It was now officially Canada's most important national emblem. And it's our pick as the #1 most outstanding Canadian symbol of all time!

MAPLE LEAF

BACKGROUND

The maple tree has played an important role in Canada's development throughout history. It contributes valuable wood products, sustains the unique maple sugar industry, and helps to distinguish the Canadian landscape. The maple's enduring abundance and usefulness make it the pride of Canada's forest land.

ANALYZE THIS!

The red maple leaf bursts with life and vitality. It is a symbolic reminder of Canada's long-standing relationship with the land and its abundant resources. The unique maple leaf also evokes the beauty of the Canadian landscape.

? What does Canada's maple leaf flag mean to you?

IT'S OFFICIAL

In the early 1800s, many newspapers and organizations began to suggest that the maple leaf become Canada's emblem. In 1860, when the Prince of Wales visited, the streets were decorated with maple leaves. After this, the maple leaf only became more popular. In 1867, Alexander Muir wrote "The Maple Leaf Forever" as a national anthem. The designs for Quebec's and Ontario's coats of arms in 1868 and Canada's royal arms in 1821 all had maple leaves. For many years, the leaf was also the symbol of the army; it was used to identify Canadian troops in both world wars. Then in 1965, the emblem received official approval: the red maple leaf flag was sworn in as Canada's new national flag.

This design, one of the finalists in the great flag debate, was the personal favourite of the then prime minister, Lester B. Pearson.

Quick Fact

From 1876 to 1901, the maple leaf was the only symbol to accompany the head of the reigning monarch on Canadian coins.

The Expert Says...

❝ [The maple] springs up tall and strong and faces the tempest and triumphs over the wind, which cannot shake it any more. The maple is the king of the forest. It is the symbol of the Canadian people. ❞

— Denis Viger, Sainte Jean-Baptiste Society of Quebec in 1834

tempest: *violent storm; unrest*

FLAG FLIERS
'proud of this country'

A newspaper article from the *Toronto Star*
By Sandro Contenta, 30 June 2007

A Canadian proudly shows off the Canadian flag on Canada Day.

At 10 o'clock Sunday morning, Philip Fournier will play a recording of the national anthem, replace the Canadian flag on his porch with a new one, and let his patriotism hang out for another year.

He performs the flag-changing ritual every Canada Day with none of the hand-on-heart dramatics so common south of the border. But his love-of-country, Fournier insists, is every bit as heartfelt.

"I've always been a patriotic Canadian," says Fournier, 56, sipping wine beneath his flapping Maple Leaf, which greets passers-by in the Riverdale neighbourhood.

"When I put it up, back in 1990, almost no one was flying the flag. I just felt we needed to show that we're proud of this country and what it stands for," he adds, citing equality and acceptance as Canada's most enduring values.

Fournier, a provincial civil servant, is part of a small minority when it comes to year-round flag waving. Canada Day officially encourages people to be loud and proud, but quiet patriotism remains the Canadian way.

Toronto flag shops, however, have noted a slight but steady increase in sales over the last few years. ...

A grateful immigrant experience is a recurring theme among flag fliers interviewed by the *Star*. Some describe sports events as the nudge for unfurling the flag. All, quite simply, say they're proud of being Canadians. ...

? Do you or your family ever fly the Canadian flag? Why or why not?

Take Note

Of all the symbols in this book, none is as Canadian as the red maple leaf. It's a symbol whose historical roots are intertwined with Canada's. It has been a part of Canadian culture and identity through the years. It's #1 on our list of the most outstanding Canadian symbols.
• Do you think the maple leaf is the most outstanding Canadian symbol? Is there another symbol that better represents or evokes Canada? Explain your answer.

5   3   2   1

We Thought ...

Here are the criteria we used in ranking the 10 most outstanding Canadian symbols.

The symbol:
- Is important to all Canadians
- Has endured through the years
- Played a vital role in the historical development of Canada
- Is well known to Canadians and the rest of the world
- Has represented Canada on the world stage
- Has helped to unite the country
- Represents universal Canadian values and ideals

What Do You Think?

1. Do you agree with our ranking? If you don't, try ranking them yourself. Justify your ranking with data from your own research and reasoning. You may refer to our criteria, or you may want to draw up your own list of criteria.

2. Here are three other symbols that we considered but in the end did not include in our top 10 list: the caribou, lacrosse, and Parliament Hill.
   - Find out more about them. Do you think they should have made our list? Give reasons for your response.
   - Are there other symbols that you think should have made our list? Explain your choices.

Index